THE
BRITISH ISLES

A Photographic Journey

Text by
PHILIP CLUCAS

Colour Library Books

THE
BRITISH ISLES

A Photographic Journey

TEXT: **Philip Clucas**

CAPTIONS: **Pauline Graham**

DESIGNED BY: **Teddy Hartshorn**

PHOTOGRAPHY: **CLB, Photo Source, Telegraph Library**

EDITORIAL: **Gill Waugh and David Gibbon**

PRODUCTION: **Ruth Arthur and David Proffit**

DIRECTOR OF PRODUCTION: **Gerald Hughes**

CLB 2625
This edition published 1993
© 1991 Colour Library Books Ltd, Godalming, Surrey, England
Printed and bound in Hong Kong
All rights reserved
ISBN 0 86283 919 X

No country in the world is richer than Britain in its patchwork of natural beauty. It is a mélange formed by the play of light and shade upon the landscape, by the tones which moss, lichen and fern impart upon mellow stonework, by the placing of spired church or ruined castle within the scene, and by the memories that have been stitched into the fabric of her landscape – into thyme-scented downland and primrose-haunted hedgerow; into silver threads of stream and darkling reed-mere.

The landscape of England, Scotland and Wales is one of rich and subtle contrast, where variety is the key to abiding fascination, and upon which each season paints its own freshness – be it the sight of wind-racked elms beyond a cornfield, poppy-studded amid the harvest gold, and shimmering in a summer's haze; the smell of wild hops hanging thickly from autumn bine; a grey winter's landscape, grizzled by sleet, its chill solitude broken only by the harsh call of the crows; or by the first flush of springtide, whose yearly appearance seems to exude the very essence of pastoral verse –

> *... When weeds, in wheels, shoot long and lovely and lush;*
> *Thrush's eggs look little low heavens, and thrush*
> *Through the echoing timber does so rinse and wring*
> *The ear, it strikes like lightnings to hear him sing;*
> *The glassy peartree leaves and blooms, they brush*
> *The descending blue; that blue is all in a rush*
> *With richness; the racing lambs too have fair their fling.*

With variety goes surprise. Britain is a country of happy surprises, and there is no need to travel far to be pleasantly astonished. In the West, among rounded hills and soft, yielding pasture, one suddenly arrives at the bleak tablelands of Dartmoor and Exmoor; and at Glastonbury there is an unexpected extent of fen whose flatness seems to suggest the landscape of Cambridgeshire. The long green walls of the South and North Downs – with their far-reaching views over the oast-houses, hop fields and orchards of Kent – are equally joyful surprises: the Weald is another of them. East Anglia has a kind of rough heath country of its own, that one never expects to find there but is always delighted to see. After the easy, rolling meadows of the Shires, the dramatic Peak District with its steep scarp never fails to astonish, for it seems to have no business there. Similarly, to the north, there are remnants of the Ice Age in the flowers and shrubs of Teesdale – Alpine gentians and juniper – whilst a short distance away drifts of bluebells, wood anemones and wild garlic carpet the primeval woodlands that crowd the vales.

Another characteristic of the British landscape is its exquisite moderation – born of a compromise between wildness and tameness. Here the hand of nature and the works of man harmonize: the hedges, the wooden fences, even the low stone walls that bind the northern fells, all have been gently subdued by nature until at last they might have been natural growths themselves, like the mosses that cover their wood and stone. Indeed, man has no need to be ashamed of the extent of his handiwork – where in Devon he built his thatched cottages of colour-wash cob, where in Herefordshire he used his timber and plaster to such striking 'magpie-like' effect, or where in the grim north he built his grey peel towers as defence against raiders from across the border. It is no accident either that the works of our earliest ancestors – such as the tall stones of Callernish, the 'Druids' Circle at Keswick, or any mighty prehistoric earthwork like Maiden Castle or Uffington Hill Fort – stand in surroundings of peerless loveliness. Thus are built (at a later age) the Abbey of Tintern on the Wye, Dryburgh in the arm of the Tweed, Rievaulx in the green cup of the Hambledon Hills, and Fountains Abbey nestled amongst trees and rocks. Of similar merit are Durham Cathedral, set high on its rock promontory overhanging the Wear, Lincoln overlooking half a county, and Ely poised triumphantly above the Fens. Nor was this sense of beauty lost with the first flush of enthusiasm – that material prosperity did not blunt the medieval mind can be seen at a glance around any Cotswold village, where houses have an irregularity and colouring that make them fit snugly into the landscape, as though they were as much a piece of natural history as the trees that shade them. Such landscapes are a comfort to man, yet the countryside has not relinquished all of its ancient savagery and power – the vast moors, the mountains and the cruel seascapes still hold him in awe.

The enormous variety of countryside to be found in Britain is what makes a journey through its landscape so infinitely rewarding. In the succeeding chapters this progression is charted, and encompasses all the regions of these enchanted Isles – from the magnificently divergent landscape of the Western shores, through the chalk downlands of Southern England, to the lush pasture and ploughland of East Anglia and the Fens. It journeys to the Cotswolds and the Malvern Hills, to the gentle terrain of the vales and the Welsh borderlands, and into the remote fastnesses of the mountains of Wales. From the Shire country of England's heartland the warmth of the South is supplanted by the rugged grandeur of Lakeland, and the cold fells and sheltered dales of the North. The final chapters cross the Cheviots and the Roman Wall to the marcherlands and Southern uplands of Scotland, which in turn melt into the full glorious fury of the Highlands, whose dramatic scenery of remote mountains, lochs and islands are the equal of any.

The West Country
Land of Contrast and Rich Diversity

It is pleasant to think of the West Country – with its long coastline abutting the surging swell of two seas and the crashing breakers of the open ocean – as though it were a country in itself. Indeed, there is a sense in which it was always so, for since man first roamed these isles the Plain of Somerset, with its all-but-impenetrable landscape of marsh and lagoon, has formed a barrier between the lands of Devon and Cornwall and the rest of England. Early lines of communication consisted of tortuous trackways which always followed the highest contour so as to avoid the steep fall of streams and the area's tidal estuaries. The trails through Somerset and Dorset, where they were low lying or progressed through forest, were virtually impassable; in some parts of these counties this remained true right up to the advent of the railways. Thus was born the West Countryman's close affinity with the wild waters of his native coastline (sea-voyage was less fraught with hazard than overland travel), forging that proud kinship with the sea that in Elizabethan times controlled the destiny of the English Realm.

Cornwall, Devon and Somerset are traditionally set apart from the bulk of England, yet these Lands of the West possess the widest diversity of scenery to be found anywhere in Britain – even within their own individual county borders. Thus are the broad, sweeping moorlands of Dartmoor, with its tors and denuded high rocks, contrasted by the mild estuaries of East Devon so close at hand. Similarly, the grandeur of Bodmin Moor to the West in Cornwall and the harsh granite cliffs of the sea-coast are the direct antipathy of the gentle 'lost' worlds where birds flash in the leaf-canopied sunlight of lanes that rise but half a mile from shore or mere. Here lies the West Country's true beauty – a beauty of informality, of secret places where sweet violets, primroses, wild garlic and flowers without number mingle with moss and damp-scented fern; where lichen-covered trees grow in woodlands haunted by stonechat, and apple trees long abandoned to nature stoop heavily under the weight of autumn fruit. Such joys are largely a matter of glimpse and chance – always of the hidden byway – and unknown to strange eyes.

The variety of the Western Landscape is due, as it is everywhere, to the geological foundation of its composition. The old red sandstone of northern Exmoor, with its rolling expanse of heath and bracken given over to centuries of wind and rain; or Dartmoor, with its peat-coloured streams that criss-cross the moor, creating areas of swamp – intensely green, yet very dangerous – bear an entirely different vegetation from the upper greensand of the Somerset Heights. These sweep down in silhouette against the southern sky to enclose wooded orchards and pastures: here the upland ash and the rhododendron flourish in profusion, and willows shed their characteristic melancholy onto the scene. It is a land of fertile alluvial plain – dotted with black-faced sheep, and ponies (the lineal descendants of the Anglo-Saxon 'wild horse') – through which silver rivers flow quietly onward to the broad surges of the bar and the everlasting thunder of the long, Atlantic swell.

Somerset is perhaps the most varied county of all. Nothing could be more perfect in contrast than the shaven slopes and lustrine cliffs of the Mendips and the rugged contours of the Bredon Hills and Exmoor – with its rounded heather knolls, the deep blue of its waters and the green woods above, where in April and early May chaffinches, wrens and willow warblers sing in coppice woodland lush with campion and royal fern. From the south of the county the frowning heights of

Blackdown look straight across Taunton Dene to the gently swelling Quantocks – filled with the souls of Coleridge and Wordsworth – and the little hills of Polden which lie below Glastonbury and the marshes of Brue.

These marshlands, now reclaimed and fertile, tell their own story of the days when Athelney and Glastonbury Tor were still islands, and when ships sailed right up the Parrett River. These lands of Alfred's exile – during Wessex' lowest fortune – have a singular dark beauty which, like the beauty of the Fens, is largely one of cloud and sky – yet the black soil and crimson osier withes give them a sinister colour – bringing back memories of Monmouth and his ill-starred confederates as though the blood of armies still stained the earth.

Of an age older than Alfred – older even than Arthur and his sword Excalibur (which is said to rest in Dozmary Pool) – is Glastonbury, which sheds the light of its legends over the surrounding marshlands. It should not be forgotten that this first Christian Church in Britain was never destroyed by the heathen invader, and that the traditions of Glastonbury stretch back to the childhood of Christ Himself; that William Blake, when he asked:

> *And did those feet in ancient time,*
> *Walk upon England's mountains green?*
> *And was the Holy Lamb of God*
> *On Englands pleasant pastures seen?*
> *And did the Countenance Divine*
> *Shine forth upon our clouded hills?*

was referring to the green Mendip Hills. Here also, according to lore, Joseph of Arimathea journeyed to the pastures of Somerset, burying the Chalice of the Last Supper – the Holy Grail – under a spring on Glastonbury Tor.

In the West Country masons had at hand everything they needed in the nature of building stone. They followed the lead of those who built so faithfully at the Abbey of Glastonbury, and all the traditional changes in architectural style – from Saxon and Norman to Perpendicular style – can be followed in the Parish churches of Devon, Cornwall and Somerset. High Gothic predominates, and many of the tallest church towers are likened to *'cold jewels set in a blaze of aquamarine that is the summer sky.'* Such are Episcopi, with its deep Norman porch, whose sandstone has been burnt red by fire, the magnificently proportioned tower of Evercrech, and the proud churches of Chewton, Mendip and Wrington.

CHALK COUNTRY
THE DOWNLAND PLAIN AND THE CHILTERNS

No matter where you wander in the Chalk Country of Southern England you will be on the downs, or on the edge of them. The Chiltern Hills range in a southwesterly direction from Bedfordshire, through Hertfordshire and Buckinghamshire, to end in Oxfordshire. Immediately across the valley of the grey-ribboned Thames the Berkshire Downs connect the Chilterns on the east with the Marlborough Downs to the west – a land of vague mists and rooks cawing above the plough. From here they run southerly to Salisbury Plain – with only the smiling valley of the Pewsey Vale to break their rolling, majestic range – from where they tumble in serried ridges into Dorset. There is a spacious permanence about this undulating landscape, where fields of feathered barley and pale green, waving wheat are interspersed by great swathes of beech-riven chalk upland, pierced only occasionally by tracts of thorn-break and briar.

It is a land of bright harvest sunshine and magnificent cloud formations. In summer it is shrouded in the rich blue of that *'unattainable flower of the sky'*, yet even on the most sultry of days there is always a breeze; and to lie on the springy turf and listen to the rustle the wind makes in the bennet is to imagine that you are hearing the whisper of some far-distant sea tide. Even when frost holds the land there is still a breeze, but so slight that all is hushed and motionless, save for the hawk that hovers and side-slips and hovers again against a slate-grey sky as it searches for prey. On such winter days as these, clouds scurry across the scene, with here and there a gleam of sunlight to flame a blackened hedgerow amber for a moment and then pass onward, to where the sun picks out the tower of a church in silver, or the gabled end of a brick-built cottage in military scarlet. Light and shadow everywhere change and exchange upon the lower chalk slopes of the hills, the evanescent sunshine clarifying small fields without number, whilst into this peace steals the sound of church bells from distant downland hamlets.

The Chalkland valleys south of Salisbury Plain are rarely more than two miles wide, and nestling in their snug folds are trees of wych-elm and oak among glades of rowan and crab apple. Ash, hazel, hawthorn and sloe stand so thickly in wayside hedges that villages are often almost hidden from sight. Valley floors are a rich alluvial deposit from which the downs rise on either side, supplanting pasture for ploughland as the soils become thinner and the white chalk breaks through. Among the water-meads of the combe, rivulets promote the growth of withy-alder, and a carpet of lush green grass (where moorhens make their nests) is spangled and starred in the first freshness of the year by innumerable wild flowers. They come to the very edge of the chalk stream – the little bluebell-like campanula, the squinancywort, the yellow bedstraw, the delicate purple scabious, the lilac-coloured rampion and the creamy-white butterfly orchis.

Topping the scarp of the chalkland district are monuments which point to the vast antiquity of human settlement within this hill-country – an area once the centre of a religion now lost to the knowledge of man. We can only speculate as to the motivating factors which prompted the raising of such incredible monuments as Avebury, Stonehenge and the awesome magnitude of the man-made mound of Silbury Hill. Less spectacular, though no less impressive, works abound in this open countryside – grey wethers and sarsens, dolmen and megaliths stand in fields and on bare downs like human figures frozen for all time, marking the route to Wiltshire's Neolithic cathedrals. From a later era the White Horse of Uffington on the sweeping Berkshire chalk points to the deification of Epona by Iron-Age Celts, who cut her sinuous form into the grassy hillside in the centuries predating Christ, when the period of the horse cult first became prominent.

Of a considerably earlier age are the hills themselves, formed during the Cretaceous period. However, unlike the chalkland of Wiltshire and Berkshire, the Chilterns are never referred to as 'downs'. They display much of the downland character but cling to their own rigid identity, the signature of which are their beechwoods – dense, silent places (as only the high woods of the Chilterns can be silent), embowered in 'Gothic' avenues of leaf, branch and sinewed trunk – bathed in the opalescent light invariably associated with the area. In springtime the Chilterns are a sea of bluebells and cherry blossom, and in early summer nightingales may be heard. Always there is the smell of beech leaves and cherry wood, and the curl of smoke ascending through trees – the blue smoke of wood fires.

The Southeast
Weald and Chalk Downland

There is nothing spectacular, there is neither the grandeur of mountains nor the sweep of great rivers to add drama to the aspect of Southeast England. It is a land of tranquil beauties; of rolling chalk downland, areas of pine and broad-leaved woodland, greensand hills rich with vegetation, little streams in wooded valleys and agricultural land of many shades – of plough, pasture and orchard. The landscape displays a harmony that is at once varied and homely – almost intimate – and peculiarly English.

The area's many different geological formations compound its diversity and have effect upon both the flora and fauna as well as the distinctive building styles of this southeastern corner of England. Not the least of its treasures are to be found in architectural features – in the little Saxon and Romanesque churches faced with chalk, tufa and split flint; in the ragstone castles of England's defensive shore, now tinged with the colour of honey by time-encrusted lichens; in Kent's cylindrical oast-houses with their red-slated roofs and wooden wind cowls, used for drying hops; in the whitewashed clap boarding of Tudor farmhouses; and in the mellow timber and brick of 18th century village cottages. To treat such a varied tract as the four counties of Kent, Sussex, Surrey and Hampshire as one unit is not an easy task, yet all have at least two features in common, which are in fact the Southeast's predominant characteristic. Firstly, there are the chalk downlands, the most significant range of southern hills which include the South Downs of Sussex and the long line of the North Downs which rise in Hampshire and traverse Surrey and Kent to end abruptly at Shakespeare's Cliff near Folkestone. These uplands, dappled in spring and summer with moving blue shadow, are bare of foliage where the chalk comes near to the surface, but trees grow in profusion wherever pockets of clay supplant the chalk. Here, beech trees predominate, forming clumps that – like the Chanctonbury Ring and the thickets at Cranborne Chase – are far-seen landmarks invariably cast into prominence by great billowing crowns of shining cloud.

Much of these rolling hills remains unwooded, yet there is compensation in the beauty of springy turf scattered with harebells and tiny heathers, and spiced with marjoram and wild thyme. It is in remote places such as these – on the windswept ridges of Southeast England – that plovers wheel above clover-scented turf cropped since time immemorial by great flocks of sheep which find pasture in the downland sheep-walks. Near their summit are trackways worn into existence by the tread of Neolithic man; and along these ancient paths are to be found dolmens, stone circles, flint workings and haunting human imagery – chalk figures incised in the turf, such as the Long Man of Wilmington and the Cerne Abbas Giant – relics of an age, more than four thousand years ago, when Salisbury Plain was the centre of a flourishing civilization. The very remoteness of such mysterious hill-top places attracted superstition, and local lore states that Woden, one-eyed and wise beyond all knowing, stalks the lonely downs wildly hunting, on black and stormy nights, for the lost souls of his ancient peoples.

Stretching between the steep escarpment of the North and South Downs lies the area's second notable feature, a wonderful expanse of woodland – much of it a relic of the great British forest of *Andred* – which comprises the Weald of Southern England. Its timber has been stripped for shipbuilding – the navy's Hearts of Oak – and for use in the numerous iron works of Sussex and lowland Kent, evidence of which can be seen in the old hammer ponds which dot the landscape. Surviving areas of the *Andred* tend to be small in extent and consist of ash, hazel, chestnut and the ever-present oak, but what these woodlands lack in scale is more than made up for by their intimate charm – by small brooks that meander through them, and by the carpet of primroses, bluebells and delightful 'wind flowers' (the wood anemone) which yearly show their blooms among the gnarled roots of great trees, struggling through briar growth and blackthorn to herald the advent of spring.

Always there are the Downs on one hand and the fertile expanse of wooded valley on the other, stretching away as far as the eye can see. In summer there is a brilliant colouring in farmland, nestling as it does beneath the chalk uplands and shielded by discreet pockets of coppice woodland. Here the rich tint of poppies growing on the margin of ploughland, in the field hedge, and on the downs themselves, bring a splash of scarlet to set off the viridian of distant hills and the flaming gold of ripening harvest. Indeed, among this lush landscape of abundance, with its orchards and pastures, nature seems to speak with the very voice of scripture -

> *Thou visitest the earth, and waterest it.*
> *Thou greatly enrichest it with the river of God,*
> *Which is full of water: thou preparest them corn,*
> *When thou had so provided for it.*
> *Thou waterest the ridges thereof abundantly:*
> *Thou settlest the furrows thereof:*
> *Thou makest it soft with showers:*
> *Thou blessest the springing thereof.*
> *Thou crownest the year with thy goodness;*
> *And thy paths drop fatness.*
> *They drop upon the pastures of the wilderness:*
> *And the little hills rejoice on every side.*
> *The pastures are clothed with flocks:*
> *The valleys also are covered over with corn:*
> *They shout for joy, they also sing.*

THE EASTERN COUNTIES
THE BROADS, BRECKLANDS AND THE FENS

The landscape of East Anglia is typically one of sweeping views, in low relief but by no means flat. It comprises areas of intense contrast: of Fenland, whose dark waters cowl sedge-swamps and reed-beds in shadowed morasses and lagoons; of estuary, mile upon mile of mud flats, and 'meals' – vast salt marshes – a lonely kingdom of wildfowl where wading birds and geese flock in their thousands. The landscape also encompasses the curious peat-dug Broadland where bitterns boom their eerie call – a labyrinth of dykes and half-reclaimed marshes – impenetrable to any but a native; and sandy heath known as Breckland, whose abiding primeval spirit is reflected in the gloomy flint-pits of Grime's Graves, quarried locally four thousand years ago. Such features are among the least spoilt of any in Britain, and are experienced to the full in wintertime, when blackened heaths and mist-haunted reed-meres reveal the solitary nature of a land racked by piercing winds driven from the North Sea.

In direct contrast to these desolate spots, the majority of the eastern counties is given over to intensive arable farmland, whose rich dark soils are numbered among the most fertile in the world. Here the landscape is entirely pastoral, swelling into gentle golden ridges, the crests of which carry hedgerows, the occasional coppice and farmsteads. This lush countryside of stream-splashed water meadows and fresh valleys has a character very much its own. It is this enchanting aspect of landscape that held one of its most famous sons in awe. For John Constable the calm of his native East Anglia held a particular fascination, *'the beauty of the surrounding scenery,' he wrote, 'its gentle declivities, the luxuriant meadow flats sprinkled with flocks and herds, its well-cultivated uplands, its woods and rivers with numerous scattered villages and churches, farms and picturesque cottages, all impart to this particular part an elegance hardly anywhere else to be found.'* If 'elegance' has perhaps changed its implication, the scene has altered little since Constable first painted it, and the Stour Valley still expresses, perhaps as completely as anywhere, the spirit of pastoral England at its best.

As with Constable's Suffolk canvases, it is the element of air and towering columns of cloud – an effect heightened by an intense vibration of light created both by the nearness of the sea and the spread of inland waters – that combine to characterise the unique quality of the East Anglian scene. Contrasting regions as diverse as Fenland and Breck, pasture and Broad, are united under the all-embracing skyscapes of the eastern counties, and each, however different from its neighbour, is evoked by that vista of open, long horizons where heaven and lonely earth seem to mingle and melt into a fusion of misty blue distance.

Throughout East Anglia water dominates the landscape – be it in the mixture of saltings, shingle ridges, sand dunes and marsh of the Norfolk coastline; or the sluggish rivers (some rising only a mile or two from the sea) which form reed-choked meres varying in nature from secluded lakelets to vast expanses, as wide as inland seas; or the fragmented marshes of the Broads, scented with meadow sweet and the sharp tang of water mint. The inconsistencies of tides have silted over harbour mouths, such as Cley, that once dispatched whalers to Iceland and ships against the Armada. Nowhere, however, does the influence of water prevail and impose itself more upon the landscape than in the Fen country of Cambridgeshire and Lincolnshire, where a million acres of rich agricultural land have been claimed by the drainage of Fenland rivers – the Great Ouse, the Nene, the Wissey and the Welland. Here, almost treeless fields are endlessly intersected by runnels which, although artificial, are in many ways one of the most distinctive features of the landscape. Fenland is a vast, flat region – much of it below sea level – upon which bad weather can induce a depression unprecedented in other surroundings, and the winter's bleakness must be experienced through long months to be realised. Yet, for all this, the Fens possess an abiding beauty – not borne of the careless English adornment of hill, stream and meadow, but one in which wide spaces and vast, restless skyscapes alter its features with each variation of weather, and demand a tribute to each changing mood.

Fenland, more than other regions, is naturally bound up with its own history. In its original state the area was an overgrown, waterlogged morass: in winter an inland sea, and in summer a swamp of stagnant meres, teeming with fish and fowl. Its few inhabitants lived on the remote patches of firm ground that stood out like islands above a clouded sea. Little wonder, therefore, that this traditional haunt of lost causes should attract the sterner monastic Orders to these remote island sites far removed from the turbulence of medieval life. Here they gradually transformed the fen into scattered settlements: green oases about their mighty churches. Such were

Thorney, Ramsey, Chatteris and Crowland – whose shattered fragments of abbeys remain – yet greatest of all, in extent and importance, is the Isle of Ely, where the Norman Minster still stands out defiantly against the violet light of the endless flats of the Great Level – the medieval flower of the surrounding domain it had conquered.

THE WEST MIDLAND VALES
THE COTSWOLDS AND MALVERN HILLS

The rolling countryside of the West-Midland Vales – a landscape of elm-fringed water meadows of the Severn and Avon, and orchards laden with damson, cherry, apple and pear – is the green heartland of England. It is the misty-green vale from which Elgar drew his music and, centuries beforehand, Langland had his vision of Piers Plowman. At its centre is the Vale of Evesham, perhaps the most productive fruit-growing district in all Britain. The land is naturally at its most beautiful at Eastertide, when its orchards are enveloped in a white foam of blossom. In pockets of wayside vegetation bluebells are found in such profusion that coppice-margins and hedgebanks are *'washed wet like lakes'* – bathed in pools of light – whose sheen continually changes as the drooping flower-heads swirl to heavily-scented breezes.

The quiet capital of its own vale, the town of Evesham arose round an abbey of which only the bell tower now survives. As with the landscape's other ecclesiastical glories, notably the medieval abbey at Tewkesbury and the cathedral towers of Gloucester and Worcester, form and construction have been meticulously honed to complement the surrounding countryside's unique qualities of light – an effect best observed (in the alliterative words of Langland's poetry), *'In somer season when soft is the sonne.'* Indeed, it is this element of luminosity – of gathering light – that best characterises the jagged Malvern Hills to the west, and illuminates the gentle, bow-headed, 'whale-back' landscape of the Cotswolds which stretch beyond the vale to south and to east.

It is here in the wold, with its predominance of honey-brown masonry, that the stones themselves appear to glow. When the limestone is first quarried it is a bleached grey, yet with the mellowing influence of time, cottages, barns and dry stone walling blush a tawny hue and acquire a radiance that marvellously merges the work of man with the spacious beauties of the surrounding hills. These are the elements that go to produce the Cotswold picture. It is a vision of undulating hillsides heaving buff-green into the distance, their thin fringes of scattered beech clear-cut against a crowded sky. It is the seclusion of valleys, lined with pollard willows, along which a clear brook threads its silver course – a haunt of lazy, dappled trout and gadding mayfly. It is a land of expansive pastures dotted with cowslip, orchis, celandine, scabious and buglewort, of hedgeside daisies and fallow fields that sweep the brow of the wold and then fall to the vale below. There are few villages to be seen, only now and then in the distance comes a hamlet, caught in a fold of hills, whose gabled stone houses with weathered stone-slate roofs reflect the sun amongst the green of moss and the yellow of lichens.

Cotswold villages are invariably strung along the course of a stream: the Windrush, the Coln, or the Evenlode, to name but a few, and each displays a careful craftsmanship and sense of style that is the particular achievement of the district. The 'Cotswold style' has remained a constant expression of local materials and need. It had its birth towards the close of the 14th century; certainly by the 15th century it had reached a high degree of maturity – as expressed by buildings such as Icomb Manor and those in the High Street at Chipping Campden. However, it is the smaller manor houses at Owlpen, Upper Slaughter, Upper Swell and Snowhill that epitomise the dignified Cotswold expression of pride in local prosperity and achievement.

A word must also be said for the churches. It is remarkable how many of these remain the primitive little structures that were raised almost a thousand years ago when the manors of the wold were first parcelled out among the Norman Lords. Though externally some of them might well belong to any medieval epoch, several (most notably at Elkstone and Hampnett) can reveal perfect Romanesque interiors hardly touched by the hand of time. The beginnings of prosperity in the 13th century – when the Cotswolds were the heart of England's wool industry – is reflected in an Early English group as typical as any in the country; North Cerney and Duntisbourne being particularly attractive, with their saddleback towers. The glory of the district is, however, the later 'wool churches' that, collectively, remain as grand a memorial to the munificence of their merchant patrons as to the genius of the masons who evoked such splendours from the resources of locally quarried limestone. Fabrics such as the Northleach, Fairford, Cirencester, Campden and Winchcombe parish churches rank with any in the land for their beauty of craftsmanship.

THE WELSH BORDERLAND
THE MARCHER HILLS AND VALLEYS

The countryside of the Welsh Borderland is possessed of a power and impressiveness – and elegance of spirit – that rivals anything that the rest of Britain can offer. Here a variety of elements, of river and dell, of orchard and swelling pasture, of woodland and hedgerow-patterned fields, mingle in a tangled complex of steep valleys and hills to produce an ensemble of sweetness and beauty.

A rural peace reigns over this landscape which spreads upwards from valley floors to the curving crests of the ridge and then drops again through skirting woods to where little rills curl among their water-meads. Seasonal colouring is everywhere apparent; in the greens and russet of bracken, in the black and purple of heather, and in the rain-soaked verdure of bent and bilberry. On a windy day it is an invigorating experience to follow the turf tracks that run along the Marcher crests, looking westwards into the wind to view the darkened, bold moorland summits, and beyond them to the azure outline of more hills (pierced occasionally by splashes of purple ploughland) and yet more ridges, backed by the profiles of the Welsh peaks. In the opposite direction lies the almost limitless expanse of the Midland Plain, heaving mile upon mile into a far distant haze. It is a prospect beloved of John Masefield. who knew well its moods and subtleties,

I have seen dawn and sunset on moor and windy hills coming in solemn beauty …

The Marcher region lies between the two great estuaries of Dee and Severn and extends southwards from Chester through the vale country of Cheshire and Shropshire (the hills and finger-ridges of the south part of that county), the tumbled plain of Herefordshire and the uplands of Monmouthshire and Dean. Along its line rise the high hills of Wales, massed in close formation – sometimes sending spurs into English soil, sometimes parting to admit green tongues of farmland into valleys threaded by swift rivers. There is a wild beauty in these vales, with their small, white, half-timbered farmhouses in magpie garb, and tumbled woods dwarfed by the austere sweeps of the heights above. Through this land from north to south the old Borderline wavers, often with an arbitrary parting of neighbouring hills, but still largely following the direction of the turf breastwork built in the 8th century by the Mercian King Offa.

The Welsh Borderland is a landscape of contrast – upland, rock formations, mountains such as the Wrekin in the west, and rich dairy pastures and grasslands to the north. At Ludlow, for example, can be seen a complete English composition, with all the traditional features of harvest cornfields and a predominance of stately trees: oak, fir and beech. In contrast, the Stiperstones are sharp and bare, with tor-like outcrops of dark rock – the haunts of kestrel and raven – or beyond to the singularly graceful peak of Corndon Hill facing sheer across country to the hedge-patterned mass of the Long Mountain and the copious triple summit of the Breidden hills.

Apart from intrinsic beauty, the Welsh Marches hold a history steeped in romance. The memory of early struggles is handed down in mighty earth-fastnesses – Croft Ambrey, Wapley, Nordy Bank – and in the husks of ruined castles such as Wigmore, Clun, Ludlow and Hopton, which stand as mute witness to centuries of turmoil and violence that abated only after the Civil War.

The subjugation of Wales was a task too formidable for direct undertaking, even by the Normans, so it came about that the Borderlands were divided out amongst the more enterprising of their soldier-adventurers, who were given *carte blanche* to build themselves fortifications from which they could conquer the wild and scattered native population. The new rulers established themselves by force, and existed in watchful defence within the confines of their so-called Lordship Marchers. Nevertheless, in the majority of cases their rule was equable, so that before long townships and villages grew up beneath Norman keeps: such were Wigmore, Hay,

Montgomery, Clun, and scores more – quiet places nowadays that seem to belong to their past, half asleep in the shadows of their castle crags. Thus, through the great medieval upheavals – the crumbling of the Llewellyn Princes, the encroachment of Marcher fiefs, the campaigning of the Plantagenets, and the culminating tragedy of Owain Glyndwr – has this wild and once remote landscape been transformed into a tract of some of the quietest and most lovely of Country Shires.

WALES
THE SPIRIT AND THE FACE

Wales is an extraordinary mixture of the obvious and the recondite, a country of romantic legends and ruined castles, yet the overpowering spirit of the landscape is one of Gothic drama – a wild, mountainous terrain of vast, indigo, cloud-misted distances, pervaded by the sound of sweet water and birdsong. Here is a depth of vision leading into the centre of an almost untouchable world of clear light and exhilarating vista – a land where curlews flock in their thousands to feed upon damp moorland, their wild plaint, at first joyous and then of long despairing lament, seems to haunt Wales eternally.

In the days of the Princes, Wales was always regarded as three entities: the Northern Kingdom of Gwynedd, The Middle Kingdom of Powis, and the Southern Kingdom of Deheubarth. Powis was never a very strong power and seldom stood by its own might; nowadays it is only a vague historical memory. Not so, however, the other two. Wales is only a unified country in the mind of the idealist – in practice it is divided into North and South. The division is precise and occurs at the River Dovey. This point is a boundary not only of Welsh feeling – between the Anglicized lands of South Wales and the spirit of Celtic individualism which has been the hallmark of the Northern lands since the 13th century – but scenery also, with the sharp mountains of the Cambrian Range lying to the north of the Dovey, whilst smoother, less dramatic mountains spread southwards across the Deheubarth landscape.

In Southern Wales history delivered a hammer blow to Welsh nationhood by the gradual inroads made by Norman Marcher Lords, who extended English conquest from the mouth of the Wye as far west as Pembrokeshire's Atlantic headland. Along this fief, part of which is still referred to as 'Little England beyond Wales', are found the ruins of the most impressive castles in Wales – Caerphilly, Manorbier, Carew, Chepstow and Llanstephan, with a host more on a lesser scale of grandeur. Everywhere along this feudal tract the Norman and English cultures dominate – fine stone houses were constructed, magnificent churches were raised, and towns on the old English plan were built. As the south coast of Wales has its line of castles stretching from the Marches to the ocean boundary, so has the Welsh northern seaboard a string of impregnable fortresses at Conway, Beaumaris, Rhuddlan, Caernarvon and Harlech – but these are of quite a different order. The former were as much baronial mansions as fortresses, whilst the latter, built by King Edward I after his conquest of Wales, were just fortified barracks for royal troops. The countryside around these bastions showed no signs of a spread of English culture and remains today as Welsh in speech, feeling and lack of architectural impulse as it ever was.

Under the yoke of Plantagenet kings the flower of Celtic independence retreated into the fastness of the Snowdonia landscape – vast mountains, notched in places like battlemented towers, with high passes and craggy peaks – from where the spirit of Welsh freedom occasionally resurfaced in the guise of her hero princes: Llywelyn the Great, Llywelyn ap Gruffydd and Owain Glyndwr. Some part of this essence of defiance seems to linger in these wild, northern mountains to haunt this highland of rock and heather, where nothing appears to have altered since the Ice Age. All is embraced by silence, save for the bleat of lambs, the sudden flight of snipe, or the solitary call of the rare red kite – described by one native poet as *'the living flame of the sky'*. Here are great, sweeping moorlands, rising to mountainous masses 2,000 feet or more in height and interspersed with marsh-flats ablaze with golden gorse flower. Views are wide and horizons far: the wind sweeps freely across the vastness, and the skylark and meadow pipit's song is lost to the breeze. However, soaring above all – dominating all – is the ethereal azure mass of Snowdon – the focus of bardic song and sentiment throughout the ages.

North Wales is a land composed almost entirely of ancient rock formations, whose contorted form and denuded surfaces were produced by ice pressure millions of years ago. In the great mass of the northern Cambrian Range, Snowdon at 3,500 feet, Carnedd Dafydd at 3,426 feet, and Carnedd Llywelyn at 3,484 feet, are sister peaks – barren on their upper slopes and in winter season snow covered – their summits reflected in lonely blue and black lakes of crystal purity set high up in their mountain folds. South and east of Snowdon, on the 2,000 feet contour, are the Arenig moorlands, the Berwyn Mountains and the Harlech Dome. These, in turn, are skirted by a rolling landscape intersected by moor and patches of peat-mire, which are almost intimidating in their sense of splendid immunity from traces of human activity – all, that is, except for an occasional ruined stone and slate cottage, the long deserted shelter of shepherds seeking the high summer pastures.

The central plateau melts into mid-Wales, and the Plynlimon group, whose characteristics are rounded grassy shapes, worn into innumerable furrows, culminating in one very definite mountain – Plynlimon. Although in height it only rises 2,465 feet, there is something very grand and distinctive about it. Plynlimon represents the cornerstone of all three provinces of medieval Wales, and also, in the peat bogs of its slopes, gives birth to both the Severn and the Wye.

Further south, along the Cambrian backbone of Wales, lie the contorted hills, tall shadowy rock gorges and great cascades of foaming water that form the Brecon Beacons. They rise to 2,906 feet at Pen y Fan and are named from their use as sites for signal fires. The wind-lashed summits have a dragonlike outline, sporting sheer precipices which fall 600 feet and have been likened to the crests of giant waves about to break into the deep valley gorges, or 'cwns' below. On either side of the Beacons are the East and West Black Mountains. They have very distinctive individualities, and it is unfortunate and confusing that they should share a similar name – even the colour is wrong, for they are composed of outcrops of red Devonian sandstone. The Eastern group – marking the end of Wales, and the beginning of England – are imposing, whale-backed barriers holding a series of long valleys, all 'blind' at the northern end. In one of these cwns is situated the beautiful, lonely ruin of Llanthony Abbey, whose monks deserted it as early as the 12th century. It was abandoned during the lawless reign of Stephen, yet to stand on its site and feel the mountains enclosing around, one wonders if it was not the overpowering nature of the savage scenery that overawed the brethren rather than the turmoil of marcher wars.

MIDDLE ENGLAND
SHIRE COUNTRY OF HEDGE AND PASTURE

One of the proudest titles attached to any area of England is 'The Shires.' This heavy, fertile land, with its flat fields and massive hedgerows, well grown elms, grazing cattle and trim farms, encompasses the counties of Middle England – notably Leicestershire, Huntingdonshire, Staffordshire, Warwickshire, Northamptonshire and the ancient county of Rutland – their wold and fen. Slow, meandering rivers and gentle, undulating countryside earn for the Shires the accolade of being considered the 'true' English Landscape – a homely attraction not easily paralleled in other lands, in other counties.

The enfolded fields of Middle England, their pastures enclosed by blackthorn and quick-set hedges, resemble nothing so much as a vast patchwork of landscape – a series of green meadows, golden in the aftermath of harvest, or brown, fawn and ochre where ploughed land has not yet yielded a crop. This is the traditional home of the grazier and the huntsman. The firm, sweet grass is widely spread and stock fatten on it and flourish as they do in few other places. Over these rich feeding grounds ride Britain's premier Hunts: the famous Belvoir (named for the ancestral seat of the Dukes of Rutland), the Pytchley and the Quorn. Indeed, the landscape might have been purposely laid out for hunting; even the woods seem tamed, used as fox coverts. The meads of this gently rolling clay country are punctuated by ash trees, put in as standards, and the majority of hedges date back to the Enclosure Acts of the Georgian Period, when thorn was inevitably used for making a fast-growing hedgerow. They offer excellent jumping and all are wide enough to hide a fox at its last gasp. Most of the great Hunts exult in grass, as does the dairy farmer, but where Middle England begins, so to speak, on the east, and the clay slopes rise from the peat of the Fens, the countryside, although rather heavy and flat, is first-class wheat and bean land. The latter crop has a singular association with the Midland landscape (somewhat similar to that of the hop with Kent), which makes the crimson flower of the runner bean a predominant colour in high summer, splashing the astonishing brightness of its bloom upon both farmland, where it bines along canes, and village and hamlet, where it outshines even the traditional cottage-garden flowers of stock, pansy and rose. The Northamptonshire poet John Clare held its beauties in high regard:

> A beanfield full in blossom smells as sweet
> As Araby, or groves of orange flowers;
> Black-eyed and white, and feathered to one's feet,
> How sweet they smell in morning's dewy hours!
> When seething night is left upon the flowers,
> And when morn's sun shines brightly o'er the field,
> The bean-bloom glitters in the gems of showers,
> And sweet the fragrance which the union yields
> To battered footpaths crossing o'er the fields.

As with the beauty to be found in the summer abundance of bean flowers, so is the landscape of the Shires best exemplified by the intimacy of its most common features. The true glory of England is its hedgerows, and nowhere is this more apparent than in Middle England. From the day when first commons and common-fields were enclosed, quick-hedges were planted. The slips were cut from hawthorn bushes that had always dotted the country and made breaks. These quicks set beside ditches – by reputation a yard deep and four feet across – grew like weeds and made the glorious paddocks and pastures that pattern the green mosaic that is today the surface of England. Within these hedgerows – now composed of holly, elder, hedge maple, crab apple and the ubiquitous hawthorn – are to be glimpsed the intimate treasures of the Shires.

At no other time of year are these 'glimpses' lovelier than at springtide, when dripping hedgebanks and rain-soaked fields are russet-brown or smokey-purple according to the play of sunlight upon the scene. The landscape is still a winter one, only flushed with spring at intervals, but birth is an imperceptible thing in nature; growth emerges quickly and suddenly in colours of misty green and grey. Its silent impetus is wonderfully evoked by Clare, writing of his native countryside:

> The dewdrops on every blade of grass are so much like silver drops that I am obliged to stoop down as I walk to see if they are pearls, and those sprinkled on the ivy-woven beds of primroses underneath the hazels, whitethorns, and maples are so like gold beads that I stooped down to feel if they were hard, but they melted from my finger. And where the dew lies on the primrose, the violet and whitethorn leaves, they are emerald and beryl, yet nothing more than the dews of the morning on the budding leaves; nay, the road grasses are covered with gold and silver beads, and the further we go the brighter they seem to shine, like solid gold and silver. It is nothing more than the sun's light and shade upon them in the dewy morning; every thorn-point and every bramble-spear has its trembling ornament: till the wind gets a little brisker, and then all is shaken off, and all the shining jewellery passes away into a common spring morning full of budding leaves, primroses, violets, vernal speedwell, bluebell and orchis and commonplace objects.

Thus were the Shire hedgerows planted, from necessity and by law, yet they have become beautiful in themselves. The oaks, ash, sycamores and elms which form the hedge standards are perhaps the most important growths in the whole landscape of these Isles.

THE NORTH COUNTRY
MOORLAND, DALES AND WOLD

Yorkshire, Northumberland and Durham were once part of the great Saxon Kingdom of Northumbria, and these wild, often windswept counties share a history as turbulent as any in Britain. In the days before industrialisation laid wide-grasping hands upon the valleys and rivers, there was scarcely a square mile of land lying between the waters of Trent and Tweed which had not some charm and beauty to reveal. But when the demand for iron-ore and coal increased as manufacturing developed, stretches of a hitherto solitary land became utterly changed in aspect and character. Fortunately, the major part of the northern landscape remains unscarred and still forms one of the largest tracts of unspoilt countryside in England.

The wolds of the East Riding, North Riding and Lincolnshire are still given over to solitude – wherein the only tenants are cattle and shaggy Swaledale sheep – and their vast distances and lonely horizons remain much as Tennyson described them,

> Calm and deep peace of this high wold,
> And on these dews that drench the furze.

The Peak country of Derbyshire is still an expanse of loveliness, and the great Yorkshire Dales remain unspoilt, their scattered, whitewashed farmsteads, dale villages and hamlets – a few cottages grouped together in a huddle of stunted trees, set far enough apart to give each an aspect of seclusion – are yet as Wordsworth knew them, lying deep and low at the foot of the high fells, each *'beneath its little patch of sky, and little lot of stars'*. Solitude, isolation from the world of industry, which is, after all, so near – these are still the prevalent characteristics of the northern dales and wolds.

Moorland, like mountain, is one of the permanencies of landscape, and has been called the 'last English wilderness'. Such a description is particularly worthy of the high, cold countryside of the Yorkshire moors and those of Durham and Northumberland, whose wide, open vistas and immense, birdswept skies are the hunting-ground of *'dapple-dawn-drawn'* falcons – the noble *'windhovers'* of the rolling plain. In summer, when moorlands 'blow' with the flowers of wild eglantine and harebells, the prevailing colour of the land is stained with the purple of heather and the yellow of vast swags of gorse and broom; yet in winter's grip – if the moors have not become interfolding acres of drifting snow and hazy blue shadow – the colour of the landscape takes on a sinister hue – reflecting the predominant granite rocks in bleak greyness, or in the browns of dead bracken. Probably the best known northern moors are those of the West Riding – at Keighley and Wadsworth – because of their nearness to the Brontë family home at Haworth. A lane near the Parsonage leads out onto the moorland where, in the stark winter weather of 1848, Charlotte set out in search of a sprig of heather, thinking it might revive her dying sister Emily. The spirit of these wild places is sombre; leaden clouds suppress the landscape, and dry-stone walling which patterns the valleys shows grey in the sunlight, and black in rain – yet under such dark cloud the moor itself turns a deep green beneath the stillness of heather and gorse.

The Pennines stretch from Derbyshire to the farthermost parts of Northumberland, and offer some of England's finest walking country. Huge expanses of upland moor – looking much as they have done since the beginning of history – sweep to a score of summits of more than 2,000 feet in the Yorkshire Dales. Over a million years ago, ice flowing down the eastward tilt of the Pennine watershed carved out the dales in their distinctive shapes. Wensleydale, watered by the River Ure, with its ravines and spectacular waterfalls of Hardraw Force and the cataracts of Aysgarth, is the broadest, most open and well-forested of the Yorkshire valleys, where tree, rock and river combine to make a prospect of rare charm. Swaledale, with its sudden twists and sinuous windings beneath its steep hills, has a more secluded grandeur, and narrower, tributary dales, such as Arkengarthdale, Bishopdale and Coverdale burrow deep between the flanks of the fells. These hills are of limestone, capped here and there by millstone grit, and upon them grow cotton grass and heather, flecked with bilberry and crowberry. There is also softer natural beauty among the rugged landscape – in the treasury of Alpine flowers left behind by the Ice Age around Teesdalehead in Durham; and in the valleys are the remains of monastic buildings that are scattered all over the Northeast: Yorkshire's Fountains Abbey, founded in 1132, is the best known, Bolton Priory ('Abbey' as it is locally, but erroneously, called) set in a wooded gorge beside the River Wharfe, and Rievaulx Abbey, which is perhaps the most romantically sited of all.

In Northumberland the Pennines merge imperceptibly with the Cheviot Hills – its moors and dales – whose remote summits command inspiring views of the Tweed gliding away to Berwick and the far sea; and beyond the river, the smiling, placid acres of the Scottish Lowlands. Walter Scott wrote of this landscape: *'The Cheviots were before me in frowning majesty; not indeed with the smiling majesty of rock and cliff which characterises mountains of the primary class, but huge round-headed and cloathed with a dark robe of russet, gaining by their extent and desolate appearance an influence upon the imagination, as a desert district possessing a character of its own'*. In the past these solitary hills were the scene of much border dispute and bloodshed, made famous in ballads such as 'Chevy Chase' which celebrates the battle between the armies of Earl Douglas and the Percys of Northumberland. These hills, which once resounded to the clash of sword and claymore in the fierce hand-to-hand fighting of the Border Wars, now echo only to the cry of the curlew. Amid the Cheviots' magnificent scenery – where star saxifrage and spring gentians are still to be found – rise the bold domes of the hills, riding across the border like massive waves.

THE NORTHWEST
LAKELAND, MOUNTAIN AND FELL

Cumbria, land of misty mountains and placid lakes, has a landscape of dramatic light and shade which possesses all the grandeur and concentrated beauty of configuration that one usually associates with the Alps. English Lakeland, with its sweeping fells and dales, is probably the most definitely bounded of all Britain's regions – lying between the massive divide of the Pennine highlands on the east and the sea coast on the west; to the north stretches the wide spread of the Solway Firth, while the silver tidal-flats of Morecombe Bay denote its southern limit. In past ages the land was densely wooded, and was so remote from the rest of England that Cumbria was looked upon as a natural part of Scotland until late Norman times. The Rey stone on Stainmoor was then regarded as the boundary marker between English and Scottish thrones – as it still is the marker between Cumbria and the rest of England.

Such rugged terrain remained empty, or nearly so, until it was populated by the last of the great migrations into Britain due to the wanderings and settlements of the Vikings, which took them to Iceland, Greenland and even to the seaboard of Newfoundland; and in Britain, to the occupation of Shetland, the Orkneys, the Isle of Man and much of Western Scotland. In the 10th century the Vikings took possession of this land of purple mountains and lakes of inky blackness, whose desolation must have appeared to them out of the mists, out of the rain, in all its ancient terror. However, the Norsemen stamped their indelible mark upon what is now called the 'Lake District', and nearly all the place names of Cumberland and Westmorland are of their tongue – *'dale'* and *'fell', 'force'* (a waterfall), *'thwaite'* (cleared ground), and *'tarn'* from the Nordic word *'tiorn'* (a tear). The Vikings are also responsible for the most fascinating relics of the district – the crosses of Gosforth and Bewcastle. The former displays a strange mixture of pagan myth and Christian symbolism, whilst the latter cross is incised in the tradition of Byzantine craft with a strength of design and power of execution that points to close links between their lakeside settlements and the distant Bosphorus, perhaps by the Viking trade routes to the Black Sea and Russia.

The region of high, windswept fells, rock crags and distant views of lofty, broken peaks, centres around the mountainous mass that culminates in Scafell and Scafell Pike – which at 3,210 feet is the loftiest peak in England. These are the spectacular images of Wordsworth's poetry:

The mountains against heaven's grave weight
Rise up, and grow to wondrous height.

Geographically, the area is the domed uplift of the earth's crust, formed by volcanic activity, which has exposed the oldest and hardest rocks at its centre – from where running water has cut dales which radiate like spokes from a wheel from the mountain knot of the Scafell crests. Later, the weight of the Ice Age worked its effect upon the landscape we know today. Sheeted thick with glaciers, the slow movement of ice cut into the valley floors, and when the warmer ages came there were deeply gouged hollows and valleys – dammed by glacial debris – into which the melting waters flowed. Here the grandeur of mountains and the bold austerity of rock crags are mirrored in the still waters of the area's myriad lakes. Among the most notable of these lakes are the lovely Ennerdale Water, Buttermere, Crummock Water, Windermere and Derwent Water – each fed by the crystal streams and rivers of this, the rainiest region in England. Their surface is of an exquisite, piercing turquoise that is not a reflection of the sky, although it may be enhanced by it just as it is changed and patterned by every breath of wind. With the wild scent of bracken and the distant whisperings of waves lapping against reeds, the English Lakes possess a calm serenity. It is the secret haunt of the Lakeland spirit – a landscape of poetic intensity – of ice-blue waters that lie placid among the heights:

> Nought wakens or disturbs their tranquil tides,
> Nought but the char that for the may-fly leaps,
> And breaks the mirror of the circling deep.

The most spectacular of the Lakes is also the deepest. Wast Water lies like a stretched silken cloth, scarcely wrinkled in the shadow of Great Gable and The Screes. With volcanic rock and sculptured, marble-like cliffs gathered on all sides, Wast Water comes closer than any other to the primitive state of glacial mere. Its waters are so exceptionally pure that it supports little wildlife – save for char, minnows and sticklebacks.

LOWLAND SCOTLAND
THE BORDERS AND THE UPLANDS

Traditionally, the southern half of Scotland is known as the Lowlands – a description which might suggest flatness and a certain lack of variety, yet nothing could be further from the truth. The Lowlands – a tableland of grassy hills and cool green pastures – stand in dignity, possessing a loveliness that is apt to be overlooked in comparison with the more dramatic splendours that the rugged Northwestern Highlands can provide. The midland valley between the Forth and the Clyde (the region's uppermost extent) is the only lowland area in the literal sense of the word; and the southern uplands rise to the Tweedsmuir Hills in the centre and the Lammermuir and Pentland Hills in the northeast. Indeed, the Scottish Lowlands are more hilly than most parts of England, and the climate, particularly in the central areas, can be as harsh in midwinter – when the first flurries of snow come scudding over the summits – as that endured by any lonely hamlet in the Highland mountains.

As always in Scotland, the most dramatic landscapes are to be found where there are hills of size; and each has its own descriptive name: 'dods' are rounded summits; 'laws' conical hills, and 'rigs' are ridges. Of the Lowland type, the most perfect specimens are to be found in the district where the Solway flats climb northwards over the watershed into Lanarkshire and the valley of the Clyde. These are not the fearsome hills of continual rock outcrop that give the mountains of the west and north their terrifying character, but gentle and wooded for the most part – where conifers and patches of green fields lie in the strath, ascending through skirting mists to where the grey mares' tails of mountain waterfalls send their drifts of spray among moss and rock-clinging fern.

The hills rise out of flat farming land, climbing among forests until, imperceptibly, the farmsteads become smaller, the rivers dwindle to brown streams, and growing crops give place to smooth, bronze-green hillsides, marked here and there with a fan of scree thrown out by an occasional winter torrent. Then the deciduous trees disappear, and in their stead is found an occasional clump of fir or a plantation of spruce, and little burns run through deep ditches cut in the soft peat. As the air grows colder and the gradient finally eases, mile upon mile of moorland can be seen, of which the particular feature is its curious, straw-brown colour, with a tarn here and there reflecting whatever colouring may be in the sky, and all the while, the cries of peesweeps and lambs emphasise the loneliness. In the far distance the landscape mingles with the ocean, and the words of Wordsworth seem to carry in the still air:

> ...a silver current flows
> With uncontrolled meanderings;
> Nor have these eyes by greener hills
> Been soothed in all my wanderings.

Where the Lowlands run into the sea there are high cliffs and remote beaches of white sand; endless vistas of foam-flecked tides reveal at the foot of every other cleft in the sea-cliff a fine old fishing village with woods about it that might have been lifted directly from remote East Anglia or the coastline of Friesland. It may be a place as big as Eyemouth – large enough to lose a score of able-bodied men in one night of storm – or it might be small and quaint and a trifle bleak, like St Abb's, perched on a promontory overlooking a harbour continually assailed by waves. It may be snug and pretty like Burnmouth, or large like Dunbar, yet these fishing communities run to type – and that a rather distinguished type – born of the constant battle between fishermen and the treacherous ocean with its fanged reefs, cross currents and sudden, violent storms.

A paradox of Scotland is that these harsh coasts are backed by agricultural land of a particularly rich quality. The fields run back from the edge of the cliffs to the hills, green and fruitful; the traditional white walls of the Scots farmsteads making delicious splashes against the monotone of pasture and land under plough. There are not many red roofs in Scotland; the common blue slate covers most of even the rural roofs, but their sombre gleaming above whitewash can make lovely effects against slopes that rise from the ploughed red soil, to where black-faced sheep and wild red deer crop the hard, thin grass of the upland, and where the golden eagle soars overhead.

In this peaceful landscape there are scars of a turbulent past: in the magnificent ruins of castles – Tantallon, Slains and Dunnottar – each overhanging the sea from its rocky crag, and in the gutted remains of great abbeys – Kelso, Jedburgh and Dryburgh – laid to waste by English invaders from the 13th to the 17th centuries. The English, however, were not the only despoilers, for there was dark treachery even among their own kind – notably by the Border reivers, or mosstroopers, and the powerful Border Earls. Wars and feuds, abduction and murder were commonplace, and 'cattle-lifters' raided to the very gates of Edinburgh, showing their contempt for royal authority. Yet out of these deeds come the tales of the 'makkars' —the poets and the 'makers' of ballads. Their stories of love and of war, often laced with sardonic wit, were told in broad Scots dialect. In the hands of the makkars – as in those of Robert Burns – this deceptively harsh-sounding language can become a tool of great beauty.

The Highlands
Mountains, Lochs and Islands

The Scottish Highlands possess the most magical and yet the most terrifying landscape in Britain. Coming up country from the border, through agricultural land full of grey stone and rounded hills, dotted with vestiges of medievalism – ruined castles and bare skeletons of broken abbeys – are seen the jagged frieze of the Grampians (the highest and largest mountainous mass in Britain) rising above the northern horizon, blue and dramatic and unmistakable. Their capacity – perhaps an effect of atmospherics – to take on at a distance a wistful, cerulean blue, characterizes all the great mountain ranges of the Scottish Highlands – the Monadhliaths, the Trossachs, the Cairngorms of the Central Heights, and the isolated mountains of the far north. These awesome ranges share the landscape with wild sea lochs that gouge deeply into the land; with icy streams that tumble through green and wooded glens; with frowning crags and darkly shadowed passes; with the calm waters of vast inland lochs and kyles and, above all, with an ever-changing sky that gives rise to an immense variety of shade and subtle hue.

Perhaps the almost excessive popularity of the Highlands is a lingering remnant of Victorian sentiment. It was certainly popularised in the minds of the public by Queen Victoria's affection for similar scenes of Deeside and the general acceptance of that romantic spirit so well encompassed by the nickname 'Balmorality'. To take this combination of pretty images; of conifers, rivers and lakes as a complete representation of the Highlands is to miss beauty infinitely more austere, profound and elusive. Indeed, it does not take any Scottish byway long to rise out of its glen to the high countryside of the mountains – through woods that degenerate into clumps of birch and hazel growing on land that hardens with every hundred feet of altitude gained, until there is only bare rock and moorland scrub. It is not a comfortable scene that meets the wayfarer's eye – but one to marvel at in all its gaunt and threatening majesty. Here is a landscape which changes from green to the brown of peat moors and the silver dazzle of spasmodic torrents fashioned fantastically by the volcanic and glacial crises of the distant past. It seems a cold and lonely place, snow-laden in the dead of winter and often assailed by driving rain, yet beauty, when it is found is – perhaps in the play of cloud-shadows on the bare, bronzed slopes, or the trail of mist across the rocky face of mountains – by its unsuspected nature all the more enchanting.

Although splendid desolation is now the motif of the Central Highlands – given over to the raven and the deer – it is as well to remember that the countryside was once the home of crofters who contrived to eke out a living from the bleak surroundings: and it is here that clansmen defended these grim passes to the point of death. At Dalwhinnie in the valley of the swift Spey the clans of old gathered in warlike array. Here they repulsed Cromwell in his day, and, more than a century later, the Hanoverian arm of General Cope. Further down the glen, near Kingussie, Ruthven Barracks were built in 1718 to keep the Highlands in check, but Bonnie Prince Charlie's Jacobite rebels destroyed them in 1746. The present desolation of these uplands is largely the result of the collapse of his cause and its ultimate destruction on Culloden Moor (surely the most drear and melancholy of all Scottish battlefields). In reprisal, crofters were forcibly evicted from their farmsteads by English troops carrying out their commission against the King's enemies. Every corner of the Highlands seems to have its touching reminder of the troubles – a ruined croft or crumbling barn – recalling the savage depopulation of the 18th and 19th centuries, when the ancestral homeland of its Celtic inhabitants was 'cleared' to make room for large scale sheep farming and English Baronial estates.

The tremendous mountain masses of the Central Heights, however imposing, are at certain seasons so hostile, so acid in colour, that their wilderness depresses rather than exalts the spirit. But towards the west the softer, more poetic light of a moister, warmer climate informs scenes of picturesque splendour with a strange and irrepressible charm. Here are found the main elements – mountains, lochs and islands – in the triumphant chord of Highland beauty. A glance at the map of Scotland reveals how freshwater lochs endlessly stud the region, and how fantastically the western coastline is indented by the sea. Here, tortuous fjords add to the scenic effect, allowing the mysteries of the oceans to send their groping fingers amid the mountains, and to fumble among the tangles of golden weed that line its shores. Near at hand the water is vivid blue, paling into a white brilliance when a burst of sunlight from the sombre sky dazzles the surface, contrasting with the green of its low isles, and, in midsummer, the yellow of cut hayfields on the far shore. Indeed, on the raw rock of mountain and on the white sands of the tideline, on pasture and on moor, the light cast by the sky and reflected by the sea plays amazing tricks of colour. In storm and in calm it combines in a thousand different ways to present to the seeing eye all the essences of Highland landscape – be it in the violet shades of distant peaks, or in the warm indigo sheen which falls upon fishing villages such as Crail, in Fife. Even Bothwell Castle in Lanarkshire has a pink wash of light at some times of day. How bathed in such light stands Iona, from where Columba started his mission and where his cathedral now abuts the western surf. Deep-cut shadows haunt the memory of Glencoe, darken the Achnashallach Forest, and fall gently across the ruins of Melrose Abbey – reputed to hold the heart of Robert the Bruce.

Previous page: Mill Bay at Land's End (above), Cornwall (these pages). Land's End marks the most westerly point on the mainland of England, with the famous mass of granite rock breaking off into the sea at the end of the Penwith Peninsula. The rocky buttress of Cape Cornwall (above left) confronts the sea not far from St. Just, the westernmost town in England. St. Michael's Mount (left) features strongly in Arthurian Cornish legend: it is said that this is all that remains of the lost land of Lyonnesse. It was from there that Tristram left to bring Iseult as a bride to King Mark of Cornwall, only to fall in love with her himself, thus providing inspiration for one of Cornwall's greatest romances. In 1044 King Edward the Confessor gave St. Michael's Mount to a Norman monastic order and a monastery was founded on the island. In 1425 the Mount was taken back by the Crown and the present castle constructed on this highly defensible site. At high tide the Mount becomes an island as the sea floods the sands and the cobbled causeway which usually link it with the mainland.

Situated on Cornwall's south coast, Polperro, despite intensive commercialization, has retained in its lime-washed houses and narrow streets all the characteristic atmosphere of an old Cornish fishing village. However, Cornish fishing villages are not necessarily very old. There is little to suggest that a fishing industry existed in Cornwall during the first part of the Middle Ages. It seems that fishing villages sprang up in an attempt to counter the economic depression that gripped England after the outbreak of the Black Death. Polperro, mentioned in records in the first half of the fourteenth century, was among the very first of Cornwall's fishing communities.

Above: the harbor of Cadgewith, Cornwall (these pages). Above left: Looe, and (left) St. Ives. The town of Looe was, until 1883, the two towns of East and West Looe. Though today the town is small and tranquil, the original two towns were once of vital importance to the nation. East Looe contributed twenty ships and 315 men to the Royal Expedition to Calais in 1346, only five ships less than London. Thereafter, however, the two towns slipped into relative obscurity with a prosperity based upon the typical Cornish industries of fishing and smuggling.

The chequered patchwork of delicate coloring at Harcombe (above) is typical of the southern landscape. Facing page: (top) Dartmouth seen from Wembury in South Devon (these pages), and (bottom) Cockington with its typical, thatched Devonshire roofs. Overleaf: Brixham Harbor. Here, in 1688, William of Orange first set foot on English soil. He is reported to have said: "Mine goot people, I mean you goot, I am here for your goot, for all your goots." Somewhat surer of the English language, Henry Lyle, vicar of Brixham's All Saints' Church during the early nineteenth century, wrote several well-known hymns, including the famous Abide with Me.

Bath, Somerset, was founded in AD 44 as an
important Roman settlement. At its heart stands
the magnificent Abbey alongside its elegant
eighteenth-century neighbor, the Pump Room.
The naturally occurring mineral waters have
continued in use for nearly all of the city's history,
since the days it was known as Aquae Sulis.

41

The Roman settlement Aquae Sulis grew up around the warm springs which made Bath (these pages), as it is now known, the most celebrated of English spas. Today the Great Roman Bath (facing page) survives as an impressive monument to Roman Britain. Above: the Pulteney Bridge. Robert Adams designed this shop-lined bridge in a Florentine style around 1777. It was named for William Pulteney, an enthusiastic improver of the city.

Above: Chipping Campden, in Gloucestershire's Cotswolds. The name "Chipping" comes from an Old English word meaning market. Chipping Campden was a wool town, prospering as early as the thirteenth century and peaking economically in the fifteenth. To the northeast of this town, in Hidcote Bartrim, lies another beautiful house, Hidcote Manor (right), Warwickshire. Above right: Longleat House, Somerset, home of the Marquis of Bath and site of his famous zoo. The house dates back to the thirteenth century when it was an Augustinian priory. Only the fishponds of that era remain, the present house being essentially Elizabethan. Capability Brown later designed the grounds. Two illustrious guests at Longleat were Charles II and Bishop Ken, the very bishop who refused permission for Nell Gwynn, the King's mistress, to stay in Winchester Cathedral Close when he was Bishop of Winchester. Charles evidently took it in good part and Ken went on to become Bishop of Bath and Wells, and was in attendance at Charles' deathbed.

Upper Slaughter, in the Gloucestershire Cotswolds. There are four theories to explain how the villages of Upper and Lower Slaughter received their strange names. One is that they were named for the sloe, which grows profusely in the area. Another is that there was once a bloody battle there, though this is thought to be unlikely. A third is that they were named from a corruption of the Anglo Saxon word slohtre, meaning a muddy place or pool. Lastly, the lords of the manor during the reign of Henry II were called de Solotres, but they emigrated to America in the eighteenth century.

The River Wye below Symond's Yat near the border between Gloucestershire and the county of Hereford and Worcester.

Left: Castle Combe, Wiltshire (these pages and overleaf), rated one of Britain's prettiest villages. It stands on Bye Brook and was built with money made from the production of cloth. Above left and overleaf: Stonehenge on Salisbury Plain. This astounding structure was erected in three phases, between approximately 2000 and 1300 BC. The stones were brought from as far afield as Pembrokeshire's Prescelly Mountains, the Marlborough Downs and Milford Haven. It is not known exactly why Stonehenge was built, but apparently its axis was built to align with the sunrise on June 21, the longest day of the year. Work was begun not by Druids, as is the popular belief, but by a people known as the Beaker Folk, agricultural invaders from the Continent. They also constructed the Avebury Stone Circle (above). This ring of stones, thought to have been constructed circa 2000 to 1600 BC, surrounds the village of Avebury. The original circle consisted of some 100 sarsen stones, sandstone boulders, also brought from Marlborough Downs. Unlike the blocks at Stonehenge, however, none of these slabs were worked. They seem to have been chosen for their natural shapes.

Left: Lulworth Cove, Dorset (these pages and overleaf). Above left: Durdle Door, and (overleaf) Man O' War Bay, both near Lulworth. Above: Corfe Castle. This building dates from the time of William the Conqueror, but the site was fortified by West Saxon kings, from Alfred onward, against the onslaught of the Danes. In 978, eighteen-year-old King Edward the Martyr received his fatal wound and appellation on this spot. His stepmother arranged his murder to clear the royal way for her own son, Ethelred the Unready. Still more foul deeds happened on this site courtesy of King John. He starved twenty-two French nobles to death in the dungeons when they supported his nephew Arthur's claim to the throne over his. Here he also imprisoned Peter of Pomfret, a hermit who predicted John's downfall. Corfe Castle eventually fell during the Civil War. Its owner, Sir John Bankes, Charles I's Chief Justice, held out against the Roundhead forces until a traitor let in the enemy. Nonetheless, the castle held out for a long time after other Royalist strongholds fell, right up until February 1646.

Swan Green, just outside Lyndhurst in the New Forest, Hampshire. This village is the cricket center for the area.

Facing page bottom: Bosham, Sussex (these pages). Here King Canute of England, Norway and Denmark vainly attempted to turn back the tide by his express command. The incident was probably legendary as Canute was known for being an enlightened monarch, unusual among Viking overlords. Fulber, Canute's contemporary and Bishop of Chartres, stated of him: "We are amazed at your wisdom and equally at your piety." The River Test (facing page top) is one of the many brooks which have carved out the chalk landscape of the South Downs. Arundel Castle (above) was built by the Norman Roger Montgomery after the Conquest to defend the valley of the Arun River against raiders. Today it is home to the Fitzalans, Dukes of Norfolk, Earls Marshal of England.

In 1834 the Duke of Devonshire inherited a small village on the south coast of Sussex and set out to create from it a rival to the nearby town of Brighton. The result was Eastbourne.

Above: Beachy Head Lighthouse, near Eastbourne, Sussex (these pages). Facing page top: the Brighton Pavilion. One writer described Brighton as "an amalgam of the raucous and the refined." The architecture of the famous Pavilion could be thought to echo that. After visiting Brighton and liking it in 1783, the Prince of Wales commissioned Henry Holland to build him a home there in 1787. The Pavilion was originally built in the "Chinese style" popular at the time, and then rebuilt by John Nash in its present Indian-Moghul style. However, the interior is still Chinese in decor. As King George IV, the Prince continued to visit regularly, and his brother, William IV, was also a frequent guest. Queen Victoria stayed here too, until she decided it did not offer enough privacy. Facing page bottom: the South Downs near Lewes.

The houses of Chilham, Kent, are largely Tudor and Jacobean, characterized by their dormer windows, projecting gables and non-linear roofs. Nearby Godmersham Park, bordering Chilham Park, was once the property of Regency novelist Jane Austen's brother Edward Knight, so she was a frequent visitor to this, one of Britain's least spoiled villages.

Facing page: the Pantiles, Royal Tunbridge Wells, Kent (these pages). The Pantiles, shaded by lime trees, is an eighteenth-century shopping walk and has changed little in appearance since the days when the town was an elegant Regency spa. Known as the Walks, it was in those days not paved but grassed. When Princess (later Queen) Anne visited there with her son the young Duke of Gloucester in 1699, he slipped on the grass and hurt himself. Anne had the town promise to pave the area over, but the town fathers neglected to do so and when she returned a year later their omission angered her. She left in high dudgeon, vowing never to return. The town hastily paved the Walks with square pantiles, hence the new name, but Anne was not to be mollified. As good as her word, she never returned. The town is relatively young, having been forest up until 1606, when Lord North discovered the chalybeate springs there. Even during its first thirty years as a spa, bathers camped out around the springs and no permanent buildings were erected. Above: Scotney Castle, Kent. This ruined, rust-colored tower was built in 1378 beside a Tudor mansion one mile southeast of Lamberhurst village.

Canterbury Cathedral, Kent, Mother Church of Anglicans the world over since Norman times. Nothing now remains of the original cathedral built on this site by St. Augustine. Indeed, most of Canterbury's pre-Conquest buildings were destroyed by the Danes. The oldest extant part of Canterbury Cathedral is the crypt, dating from 1100. Only one English monarch is buried in the Cathedral. Henry IV lies beside his wife, Joan of Navarre, in the Trinity Chapel. Also in Trinity Chapel, of course, is the Shrine of St. Thomas à Becket, Archbishop from 1162 to 1170. He was the "turbulent priest," murdered by four knights of Henry II and his shrine was the object of pilgrimages for more than 300 years, until it was wrecked and plundered by Henry VIII. Indeed, Chaucer's poem Canterbury Tales centers around one such pilgrimage to his shrine.

Right: Abinger Hammer, Surrey. Running through this village is the Dorking-Guildford road, a main thoroughfare which passes under the famous village clock. This is inscribed, appropriately, with the words: "By me you know how fast to go." The figure of a blacksmith strikes the hours. That and the word "hammer" in its name signify that the village was once part of the region's prosperous iron-forging industry. Nearby, in 1873, Bishop Wilberforce, son of the great reformer William Wilberforce, was killed in a riding accident. Overleaf: the River Thames seen from Richmond Hill, Richmond, Surrey.

Derby Day, Epsom Downs, Surrey. The English
Derby is one of the most famous horse races in the
world, and Epsom Downs probably one of the
most famous courses. The first derby was run in
1780 and was named for the Earl of Derby, who
was evidently a keen horseman – another famous
race inaugurated a year previously had been
named the Oaks after his ancestral home.

Facing page: Big Ben and the Houses of Parliament, formally known as the Palace of Westminster, in the City of Westminster, London (these pages and overleaf). Big Ben, a 320-foot-tall clock tower, contains a 13.5-ton bell named after the First Commissioner of Works, Sir Benjamin Hall. Top: Tower Bridge over the Thames, built by William the Conqueror, and (above) Buckingham Palace seen from the Mall. "Buck House," as it is affectionately known, was built in 1703 by the Duke of Buckingham and sold to George III in 1762. Victoria was the first monarch to live there. Overleaf: Trafalgar Square with Nelson's Column at its center.

Above: the Houses of Parliament, London (these pages). Top: the Bank of England. Facing page: Saint Paul's Cathedral. The Cathedral's architect, Sir Christopher Wren, was the first person to be buried here when he died aged ninety-one. His tomb is inscribed with the words "If you seek my memorial, look about you." It took him thirty-five years to build Saint Paul's and, astoundingly, this monumental church withstood the battering of the Blitz during the Second World War, becoming an inspiration to war-wrecked London. Bombs fell all around, to the right and left, but none destroyed Wren's great church.

This page: Windsor Castle, Berkshire. This is the largest inhabited castle in the world, covering thirteen acres. William the Conqueror had it built in its strategic position, and since then almost every monarch has added to or altered the building. Facing page: Hampton Court, Surrey. This magnificent Tudor house, begun in 1514, was designed and built on the north bank of the River Thames by Cardinal Wolsey. With his fall from favor over the Anne Boleyn affair he made a "gift" of it to Henry VIII, who enlarged it as his favorite residence. Five of his wives were installed here and it is said that the ghosts of two of them, Catherine Howard and Jane Seymour, still roam its corridors. It would have taken the King four hours to get by boat from this palace to Westminster.

Blenheim Palace in Woodstock, Oxfordshire, is the grandiose masterpiece of Sir John Vanbrugh, built for John Churchill, the First Duke of Marlborough. It was built over three acres between 1705 and 1722 and the park was first laid out by Henry Wise, gardener to Queen Anne. Sarah Jennings, Churchill's wife, had been the Queen's favorite companion before she was crowned in 1702, so not only was Sarah given the use of the Queen's gardener, but she acquired her husband's dukedom for him. The enormity of this Versailles-like palace was summed up in some couplets by Alexander Pope: "'Thanks, sir" cried I, 'tis very fine | But where d'ye sleep or where d'ye dine? | I find by all you have been telling | That 'tis a house and not a dwelling."

Merton College, Oxford University, seen from Christchurch Meadows. Merton is one of Oxford's oldest colleges, founded in 1264 by Walter de Merton, Bishop of Rochester. The old city wall still encloses part of the college. Overleaf: the War Memorial Gardens of Christ Church Hall, Christ Church College. Christ Church was founded by Cardinal Wolsey in 1525 and its college chapel, originally the Church of St. Frideswide, is the cathedral of the diocese.

The Royal Henley Regatta on the River Thames. The Regatta has brought more fame to the Oxfordshire town of Henley-on-Thames than anything else. The first inter-university boat race was held here in 1829 and within ten years it was firmly established, attracting splendid prizes from willing patrons. One of the Regatta's keenest patrons was the Prince Consort, Albert, who bestowed upon it the title Royal Henley Regatta.

Above: Thorpe St. Andrew, near Norwich in Norfolk. Top: the Floral Clock, Great Yarmouth, Norfolk. In 1820 Anna Sewell, authoress of Black Beauty, *was born in this town. John Constable, the famous painter of rural scenes, was born in Suffolk and educated at Lavenham (facing page), one of the loveliest of Suffolk wool towns with many of its old medieval timber houses still intact. Overleaf: King's College, Cambridge University. This magnificent building was started under Henry VI in 1441. The chapel was begun in 1446.*

Left: the Royal Shakespeare Theatre, Stratford-upon-Avon, Warwickshire (these pages). The theatre was endowed by Charles Edward Flower, the brewer. Stratford is, of course, most famous as the birthplace, circa April 23, 1564, of William Shakespeare. He is buried in the same church in which he was baptized, Holy Trinity Church. In 1582 he married Anne Hathaway, who was eight years his senior. While he worked and lived in London, she stayed in Stratford with their children. Above: Anne Hathaway's Cottage, Shottery, near Stratford. Above left: Welford-on-Avon.

Facing page: the Pass of Llanberis through Snowdonia Heights, Wales (these pages). Above: the mountains of Caernarvonshire, rugged neighbors of Snowdon. It is small wonder, looking at the wildness and ruggedness of this terrain that Felicia Hemans was inspired to write of Wales: "Eryri! temple of the bard! | And fortress of the free! | 'Midst rocks which heroes died to guard | Their spirit dwells with thee!"

The Easter Rising of 1916 from the General Post Office (above), on O'Connell Street (these pages),
Dublin, Eire, resulted in much of the street's east side being destroyed. Bullets even chipped at John
Henry Foley's statue of Daniel O'Connell (facing page top), "The Liberator," which stands on the
north side of O'Connell Bridge over the River Liffey.

Caherconree Mountain (above) in County Kerry, Eire, is 2,713 feet high, one of the tallest in the Slieve Mish Range. Above right: the hills and plains of County Cork, Eire. Right: Benbane Head, east of the Giant's Causeway, County Antrim, Northern Ireland.

Derwent Water, the Lake District. This beautiful lake inspired Constable to paint Storm Over Derwentwater, Evening *in 1806, a soft, lyrical painting that acts almost as an illustration of Wordsworth's description of the place.*

Facing page: Ullswater, the Lake District (these pages), Cumbria. This was an area William Wordsworth knew well. It was near here that he wrote his famous lines on daffodils. In another poem The Sonambulist he begins "List, ye who pass by Lyulph's Tower ..." Lyulph, or L'Ulf, was thought to be a baron or chieftain who built the original tower near the lake. Ullswater is believed to have derived its name from his. Above: Sphinx Rock on Great Gable.

Above: a farm near Bransdale, North Yorkshire (these pages and overleaf). Overleaf: Whitby Harbor and St. Mary's Church – the River Esk empties into the North Sea at Whitby, hence the thriving fishing industry. St. Mary's stands atop 199 steps near the ruins of an abbey which was founded by St. Hilda in 657. It was destroyed by Danes in 867.

Above: Edinburgh Castle, seen from Princes Street. Facing page: (top) a view of Edinburgh from Calton Hill, and (bottom) the Castle, perched on volcanic rock, overlooking Princes Street, the Old Town and the Firth of Forth far in the distance. Edinburgh, Scotland's historic capital, is often referred to as the Athens of the North because it flowered into a world-renowned cultural center during the eighteenth and nineteenth centuries. Among the many famous figures who have lived here are writers Robert Burns, James Boswell and Sir Walter Scott; philosopher David Hume; political economist Adam Smith; painter Sir Henry Raeburn, and engineer Thomas Telford.

Above: the River Beathach at Glen Orchy, Scotland. Facing page: the Pass of Glencoe, or the Glen of Weeping. Historian Macaulay described this pass as "the most melancholy of all the Scottish passes – the very Valley of the Shadow of Death." He was, of course, referring to the massacre of 1692 when a company of soldiers under Robert Campbell as commander murdered more than forty Macdonalds who had entertained them hospitably for twelve days – the memory of which taints the region with the air of treachery and infamy to this day. The Macdonalds had refused to renounce the Jacobite cause and swear allegiance to William III by the date set by the English government. The order for the savage attack is said to have been written on a playing card – the Nine of Diamonds – known ever since as the Curse of Scotland.

Above: the Glencoe massif, and (left) Loch Achnacarry. Above left: the peaks of Ben Lui by the village of Tyndrum in Glen Lochy. The baronial Inverary Castle (top left) on Loch Fyne in Strathcylde is the heraldic seat of the Dukes of Argyll and the headquarters of Clan Campbell since the early fifteenth century. Dr. Johnson was entertained here by the 5th Duke while he traveled around the Highlands with Boswell in 1773.

119

Ranged along the sheltered inlet of Loch Carron is the fishing hamlet of Plockton (above), flanked on the north by the Applecross mountains, which appear to rise from the waters of Loch Torridon. Right: the paddle steamer Waverley *churning the waters of the Kyles of Bute. Above right: yachts on Loch Leven, Scotland (these pages). Mary Queen of Scots was imprisoned in Loch Leven Castle, but she made a spectacular escape with the help of William Douglas.*

The Highland castle of Eilean Donan stands sentinel at the confluence of Lochs Duich, Alsh and Long in Scotland.

Inverlochy Castle (above), beneath the intimidating mass of Ben Nevis, retains the ancient name of the nearby town rechristened Fort William after the first Scottish rising of 1715. Above right: Inverary Castle on Loch Fyne, and (right) Balmoral Castle, Aberdeenshire, the Royal Estate. The castle was the inspiration of Albert, Prince Consort, who supervised its construction after his purchase of the estate in 1852.

Right: Glenfinnan at the head of Loch Sheil, Scotland (these pages and overleaf). The statue of Prince Charlie commemorates his raising of the Jacobite standard on this spot on August 19, 1745. It is inscribed, "a throne lost by the imprudence of his ancestors." It was erected in 1815 by Macdonald of Glenaladale, the grandson of one of the Prince's original supporters. Overleaf: Loch Creran in Argyllshire.

REGISTER